WOMEN
GROUNDBREAKERS

WOMEN IN SCIENCE

Miriam Coleman

PowerKiDS
press.

New York

Published in 2016 by The Rosen Publishing Group, Inc.
29 East 21st Street, New York, NY 10010

First Edition

Editor: Sarah Machajewski
Book Design: Reann Nye

Photo Credits: Cover (background) Sofiaworld/Shutterstock.com; cover (Goodall) GREG WOOD/AFP/Getty Images; cover (Curie) Forum/Universal Images Group/Getty Images; cover (Carson) Alfred Eisenstaedt/ The LIFE Picture Collection/Getty Images; p. 5 http://commons.wikimedia.org/wiki/File:Florence_Bascom2.jpg; p. 7 (inset) http://commons.wikimedia.org/wiki/File:Mary_Anning_Plesiosaurus.jpg; p. 7 (Anning) http:// commons.wikimedia.org/wiki/File:Mary_Anning_painting.jpg; p. 9 Hulton Archive/Hulton Archive/ Getty Images; p. 10 Popperfoto/Popperfoto/Getty Images; p. 11 http://commons.wikimedia.org/wiki/ File:Entrance_to_Musee_Curie,_Paris.jpg; p. 13 http://commons.wikimedia.org/wiki/File:Chien-shiung_Wu_ (1912-1997).jpg; p. 15 (Villa-Komaroff) Boston Globe/Getty Images; p. 15 (background) Spaces Images/ Blend Images/Getty Images; p. 17 WILL & DENI MCINTYRE/Science Source/Getty Images; pp. 19, 21 CBS Photo Archive/CBS/Getty Images; p. 23 ATTILA KISBENEDEK/AFP/Getty Images; p. 25 BERTRAND GUAY/AFP/Getty Images; p. 27 Jemal Countess/Getty Images Entertainment/Getty Images; p. 29 anyaivanova/Shutterstock.com.

Library of Congress Cataloging-in-Publication Data

Coleman, Miriam, author.
 Women in science / Miriam Coleman.
    pages cm. — (Women groundbreakers)
 Includes bibliographical references and index.
 ISBN 978-1-4994-1047-1 (pbk.)
 ISBN 978-1-4994-1077-8 (6 pack)
 ISBN 978-1-4994-1086-0 (library binding)
 1. Women in science—Juvenile literature. 2. Women scientists—Juvenile literature. I. Title.
 Q130.C65 2016
 305.43'5—dc23
                              2015006140

Manufactured in the United States of America

CPSIA Compliance Information: Batch #WS15PK: For Further Information contact Rosen Publishing, New York, New York at 1-800-237-9932

CONTENTS

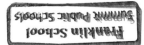

BREAKING THROUGH

When Florence Bascom was pursuing her **Ph.D.** in geology from Johns Hopkins University, she had to sit behind a screen so the men in her classes wouldn't know she was there. In 1893, she became the first woman to receive a Ph.D. from Johns Hopkins.

Bascom later became the first woman geologist hired by the U.S. Geological Survey, the first woman to present a paper to the Geological Society of Washington, and the first female officer of the Geological Society of America. Like many women throughout history who chose careers in science, Bascom had to overcome **obstacles** to rise to the top of a field controlled by men. By showing she had skills to match the men in her field, Bascom helped pave the way for future generations of female scientists.

AMAZING ACHIEVEMENTS

Bascom founded the department of geology at Bryn Mawr College and taught there until 1928. At least three of her female students went on to work for the U.S. Geological Survey.

Science was once known as a "man's world." However, female scientists throughout history and today have proven otherwise.

THE FOSSIL HUNTER

Mary Anning was born in 1799 in Lyme Regis, a seaside town on the southern coast of England. The cliffs and shores near her hometown were rich with fossils, and Anning's father taught her how to collect them when she was young. After her father died, Anning and her family collected and sold fossils to earn money.

When Anning was only 10 or 12 years old, she and her brother discovered remains of an *Ichthyosaurus* dinosaur—the first of its kind known in England. She soon developed a rare talent for fossil collecting and, without any formal education, taught herself the scientific subjects she needed to identify the creatures she found. Her discovery of the first *Plesiosaurus* dinosaur in 1823 and countless other fossils helped scientists understand what the world was like more than 150 million years ago.

AMAZING ACHIEVEMENTS

Because Anning was a woman and poor, many people did not take her skills and knowledge seriously. However, she has been called "the greatest fossilist the world ever knew."

One scientist thought Anning's drawing of the *Plesiosaurus* was fake. However, the find was real and made the Anning family respected in the field of **paleontology**.

A BRILLIANT PARTNERSHIP

In 1891, 24-year-old Marie Sklodowska traveled to Paris to study **physics** and mathematics because only men were allowed to attend college in her native Poland. While there, Marie met fellow physicist Pierre Curie. They married and soon became partners in the investigation of **radioactivity**. Together, through careful yet difficult laboratory work, the Curies discovered the radioactive elements polonium (named for Marie's homeland) and radium.

Marie realized rays from these radioactive elements glowed and that this property came from an element's atomic structure. This discovery helped create a new branch of science called atomic physics. In 1903, Marie and Pierre Curie, along with another scientist named Henri Becquerel, were awarded the Nobel Prize in Physics for their work on radioactivity. Marie Curie was the first woman to receive this **prestigious** award.

After high school, Marie Curie took classes in secret. She worked as a tutor in Poland for five years and studied physics, chemistry, and math in her spare time.

Marie Curie

AMAZING ACHIEVEMENTS

Marie Curie's daughter followed in her mother's scientific footsteps. In 1935, Irène Joliot-Curie and her husband, Frédéric Joliot, won the Nobel Prize in Chemistry for their work on new radioactive elements.

In 1906, Pierre Curie died after accidentally stepping in front of a horse-drawn wagon. Marie took over his teaching position at the Sorbonne, becoming its first female professor. She continued her work on radioactivity and in 1911 received another Nobel Prize, this time in chemistry. She became the first person to win the Nobel Prize twice and the only woman to win it in two different fields.

Curie used her work to develop treatments for wounded soldiers in World War I. She also founded the Institut du Radium for the study of radioactivity and nuclear physics, which helped pave the way for other female scientists. Unfortunately, Curie's work with radioactive chemicals seriously affected her health. She died in 1934.

Today, the Institut du Radium is a museum open to the public. Visitors can learn about Curie's life and the important breakthroughs she made, not just in science, but also for women.

THE FIRST LADY OF PHYSICS

Dr. Chien-Shiung Wu came to the United States from China in 1936. A brilliant student, she was traveling across the world to study physics at the University of California, Berkeley. After earning her Ph.D., Dr. Wu was recognized as an expert in **nuclear fission**. She became a physics professor at Columbia University, where she also conducted research.

During World War II, Dr. Wu worked on the Manhattan Project. This was a secret program to develop the atomic bomb for the U.S. Army. She helped invent a process that produced large amounts of fuel for the bomb. In 1957, Dr. Wu helped disprove an accepted law of symmetry in physics. Dr. Wu's male **colleagues** received the Nobel Prize in Physics for the discovery, though she did not.

AMAZING ACHIEVEMENTS

Dr. Wu received the National Academy of Sciences' Cyrus B. Comstock Prize in 1964, the U.S. National Medal of Science in 1975, and the 1978 Wolf Prize in Physics. She was also the first Chinese American elected to the National Academy of Sciences. She is known as the "First Lady of Physics."

Dr. Wu often gave talks about what it was like to be a woman in a male-**dominated** field. She hoped she could inspire girls and young women to pursue careers in science, technology, engineering, and math.

BREAKING BARRIERS

Lydia Villa-Komaroff is one of today's leading scientists. However, when she graduated with a Ph.D. in science in 1975, she was only the third Mexican American woman in the United States to have done so.

Villa-Komaroff's love for science began at an early age. She studied it in college, but the road wasn't easy. In her first year, Villa-Komaroff's academic advisor told her women didn't belong in chemistry. Villa-Komaroff's accomplishments have proven otherwise.

In 1978, Villa-Komaroff led a team that discovered how to make insulin, an important chemical in the human body, from bacteria. Since then, she's worked as a professor, researcher, and as the chief scientific officer of a major research company. Today, she inspires women of all backgrounds to achieve their dreams.

AMAZING ACHIEVEMENTS

Villa-Komaroff was a straight-A student until college. She actually failed many important college science classes! However, she says hard work and discipline helped her turn her grades around.

Science is a field in which women—especially women of color—are underrepresented. Role models like Villa-Komaroff prove that a career in science can be earned by anyone willing to work hard.

BATTLING DISEASE

Gertrude Elion had trouble finding a job after earning her bachelor's degree in chemistry at age 19. It was the 1930s, and most laboratories at the time wouldn't hire women as chemists. Elion eventually found part-time work as a lab assistant. She continued her education and earned a master's degree in 1941.

Elion began working towards her Ph.D., but got a job with a pharmaceutical, or drug, company, where she studied **viruses**. She put her studies on hold to focus on her work there. Her work led to important new methods and drugs to treat sicknesses such as leukemia and AIDS. In 1988, Elion, along with her colleagues George H. Hitchings and James W. Black, received the Nobel Prize in Medicine.

AMAZING ACHIEVEMENTS

Gertrude Elion left school before getting her Ph.D., but many universities awarded her honorary doctorates throughout her lifetime.

Elion was the first woman admitted to the National Inventors Hall of Fame in 1991.

A WAY WITH WORDS

Rachel Carson was a talented **marine biologist**, but her gift for writing brought her work to many people and changed the way people treat nature. After studying at the Woods Hole Marine Biological Laboratory and earning her master's degree in **zoology** from Johns Hopkins University in 1932, Carson began writing radio scripts for the U.S. Bureau of Fisheries. She also wrote articles on natural history for the *Baltimore Sun*.

Carson eventually became editor in chief of all publications for the U.S. Fish and Wildlife Service. Her first three books, *Under the Sea-Wind*, *The Sea Around Us*, and *The Edge of the Sea*, helped teach the public about life in the ocean. Her writing was known for showing people how humans are a part of nature.

Carson became a full-time nature writer in the 1950s. Her first three books were all best sellers.

Carson had always worried about the ways people polluted the **environment**. In 1962, she wrote about the harmful effects of chemicals in a book called *Silent Spring*. She showed how attempts to get rid of insects with chemicals such as DDT were hurting the entire food chain—from the leaves on the trees to birds and even humans.

Chemical companies were unhappy with the book and threatened to sue Carson. They tried to say she was unscientific and even criticized her for being an unmarried woman. A government investigation, however, proved she was right, and DDT was banned in the United States. Carson's work inspired the modern environmental movement and led to the formation of the U.S. Environmental Protection Agency, Greenpeace, and Friends of the Earth.

AMAZING ACHIEVEMENTS

Carson was awarded the Presidential Medal of Freedom in 1980–16 years after her death.

Rachel Carson, pictured here in 1963, gives a TV interview about *Silent Spring*.

LIVING WITH CHIMPS

Jane Goodall's interest in animals began at a young age, when she observed the chickens at her family's home in England. She always dreamed of going to Africa to see its wildlife. She made it there when she was 23 years old.

Goodall had no formal scientific education when she made her first major discovery. She had been working as an assistant and secretary to a scientist in Kenya, who sent her into the forests of Gombe Stream National Park in Tanzania to study wild chimpanzees in 1960. After months spent closely watching the chimps, she observed that they made tools out of twigs in order to hunt for termites. Until that time, scientists thought humans were the only creatures that made tools.

AMAZING ACHIEVEMENTS

Goodall earned the trust of the chimps she was observing by imitating them, eating the same kinds of food, and hanging out in trees. This allowed her to get closer to the animals and learn more about them.

Early in her career, Goodall was criticized for giving the chimpanzees she studied names instead of numbers, which scientists felt was more scientific.

Goodall went on to earn a Ph.D. in ethology, which is the study of animal behavior, at Cambridge University. She also started the Gombe Stream Research Center to train other scientists to study wild chimpanzees. The research at Gombe showed how much chimpanzees have in common with humans, such as having emotions and personalities. Studying what ties apes and humans together has led to a greater understanding of what makes us human.

Goodall also came to realize that the African forests where these apes lived were being destroyed and that chimpanzees were in great danger. Through the Jane Goodall Institute, she focuses on keeping chimpanzees and other wildlife safe and educating young people around the world about the importance of protecting nature.

In one of her books, Jane Goodall wrote this message to young readers: "The most important thing I can say to you . . . is that you, as an individual, have a role to play and can make a difference."

A WOMAN OF FIRSTS

Shirley Ann Jackson began some of her earliest science experiments on honeybees when she was just eight years old. As she grew older, she became interested in physics. In 1973, Jackson became the first African American woman to receive a Ph.D. from the prestigious Massachusetts Institute of Technology. She later held many research positions at AT&T Bell Laboratories, where she helped achieve advances in telecommunications.

In 1995, President Bill Clinton appointed Jackson chairman of the U.S. Nuclear Regulatory Commission. This put her in charge of protecting the nation's public safety and security as well as the environment. She was the first woman and the first African American to hold the position. Today, she's the president of Renesselaer Polytechnic Institute, which is one of the top-ranked research universities in the United States.

Jackson gives a speech during an event about education in 2012.

AMAZING ACHIEVEMENTS

Discover Magazine named
Jackson one of the "top 50
women in science" in 2002.

PASSING THE TORCH

The history of science is full of tales of women overcoming obstacles and making scientific breakthroughs. Many of the women who beat the odds to succeed in science worked to make their field more open to women. Pioneers such as Rachel Carson, Shirley Ann Jackson, and Marie Curie all made education an important part of their career and helped future generations of women take the lead in their field.

More women are studying science and pursuing it as a career than ever before. Since the late 1990s, women have been earning about half of all bachelor's degrees in science and engineering. Although they still may be outnumbered by men, young women in science today can look to a long line of brilliant groundbreakers for inspiration.

Whether they're in the lab or out in the field, there are many jobs for women in science.

TIMELINE OF WOMEN IN SCIENCE

1811 - Mary Anning and her brother uncover the first *Ichthyosaurus* known in England.

1843 - British mathematician Ada Lovelace writes what is considered the first computer program.

1847 - American Astronomer Maria Mitchell discovers a comet.

1896 - Florence Bascom becomes the first woman geologist hired at the U.S. Geological Survey.

1903 - French-Polish chemist and physicist Marie Curie becomes the first woman to win the Nobel Prize.

1911 - Marie Curie becomes the first person to win the Nobel Prize twice.

1935 - Irène Joliot-Curie and Frédéric Joliot win the Nobel Prize in Chemistry.

1945 - The U.S. Army hires five women to program the Electronic Numerical Integrator and Computer to perform military calculations during World War II.

1951–1953 - British molecular biologist Rosalind Franklin uses X rays to photograph the structure of DNA.

1957 - Chinese American physicist Chien-Shiung Wu helps disprove an accepted law of symmetry in physics.

1960 - Jane Goodall begins her study of chimpanzees in Tanzania.

1978 - Lydia Villa-Komaroff leads a team that discovers how to make insulin from bacteria.

1983 - American geneticist Barbara McClintock becomes the first woman to win the Nobel Prize in Medicine.

1984 - French virologist Françoise Barré-Sinoussi helps isolate HIV, which is the virus that causes AIDS.

1988 - Gertrude Elion is awarded the Nobel Prize in Medicine.

1995 - American physicist Shirley Ann Jackson is appointed chair of the Nuclear Regulatory Commission.

GLOSSARY

colleague: A coworker.

dominate: To be the biggest part of something.

environment: The surroundings in which animals and plants live.

marine biologist: Someone who studies life in the sea.

nuclear fission: The splitting of the nucleus of an atom, resulting in the release of great amounts of energy.

obstacle: Something that blocks one's way.

paleontology: The study of animal and plant fossils.

Ph.D.: The highest-level college degree. People who earn this degree hold the title of "doctor."

physics: A branch of science concerned with matter and energy.

prestigious: Having high status.

radioactivity: A property possessed by some elements of letting out dangerous energy in the form of waves.

virus: A very tiny thing that can cause illness when it enters the body.

zoology: The study of animals.

INDEX

WEBSITES

Due to the changing nature of Internet links, PowerKids Press has developed an online list of websites related to the subject of this book. This site is updated regularly. Please use this link to access the list: www.powerkidslinks.com/wmng/sci